GW00601740

South Coast Landscapes

JO DARKE

South Coast Landscapes

B T Batsford Ltd · London

©Opus Books 1983
First published 1983

ISBN 0 7134 4189 5

Typeset by Typewise Limited, Wembley
and printed in Hong Kong

Produced in co-operation with
Opus Books and published by
B. T. Batsford Ltd
4 Fitzhardinge Street
London W1H 0AH

CONTENTS

LIST OF ILLUSTRATIONS

Introduction

From Dover to Plymouth the headlands, havens and holiday beaches of seven counties are lapped by the waters of the English Channel along the 400-mile span of England's south coast. The coastline stretches from Kent's eastward shoreline to the sleepy estuaries of the far South West, where the Cornish border marks an ancient dividing line between Alfred's Wessex and Celtic Britain.

The French call the English Channel *La Manche,* meaning 'The Sleeve', and on the English side the sleeve has a strikingly beautiful cliff line which includes the chalk heights of England's southern downs, the dark Jurassic clays of Dorset and the Red Sandstone of Devon. In the south coast's colourful past occurred some of the most significant and momentous events of English history, from Julius Caesar's arrival in 55BC to the D-day embarkations of 1944 when over a period of 14 months more than three million servicemen, British and American, set out for Normandy from Southampton alone. Since those times the south coast no longer lives on the alert against invasion from Europe, and in this age of leisure we can enjoy the architecture of cliffs and towns by road or by path or, like that seafaring essayist Hilaire Belloc, 'threading out of harbours, taking the mud, trying to make further harbours, failing to do so, getting in the way of more important vessels…anchoring in the fairway, getting cursed out of it, dragging anchor on shingle and slime, mistaking one light for another, rounding the wrong buoy, crashing into other people….' But whichever route we take, there unfolds a fabulous pattern of coastal scenery and architecture often marred since Belloc's time but otherwise expressed in white turf-topped cliffs, harbours, castles, lonely marshes haunted by boats and birds, and the graceful Regency seafronts of seaside resorts. Wonderful panoramas from piers or headlands show sweeping variations in successive rock formations where the cliffs change from clays to limestones to chalk; or the contrasts are sometimes revealed in a single cliff face. In Alum Bay on the Isle of Wight, bands of sandstone laid down on the beds of primaeval oceans have been uptilted during some later earth movement, the cliffs there showing stripes of reds and yellows and browns – a scenic marvel completed by weird chalk pinnacles, the Needles, standing off the windy chalk downs to which they once belonged.

The Isle of Wight is a magical island with its own miniature and varying landscape, and each of the south coast's counties lends its singular character to the coastal scene. A distant windmill standing on inland cliffs between Hythe and Hastings gives the hint that we have entered Sussex, while a red sail sliding between fields and trees of a river estuary sets the scene on Devon's shores. Yet since the English Channel was carved, in the aftermath of the Ice Age, the Channel waters have continued to shape our southern coastline. Cliffs are eroded by wave action, and shingle is heaped up along storm beaches like Slapton Sands in Devon or the Chesil bank in Dorset, and on the shingle promontory of Dungeness in Kent. In medieval times terrible storms washed away whole towns which finally, rebuilt, were marooned inland by the accumulation of shingle and the gradual retreat of the sea. Thousands of years before this, the coast was changing on an even greater scale. The Isle of Wight's chalk downs that reach across its width once extended westward to form a

First sight and last memory of Britain: Dover's famous white cliffs where southern England's chalk downlands reach the sea.

continuous range with the Purbeck Hills, and the river Frome which runs eastward past Dorchester to emerge at Poole Harbour was once held within the arm of these lost hills. Land stretched far south of the present Hampshire basin: fed by tributaries from north and south, the Frome flowed along what is now the Solent and through Spithead to reach the sea at a point south-west of the Wight. As the sea encroached and flooded this river system, it filled the deep tongue of Southampton water and created a channel which in later ages would accommodate great Venetian galleys carrying wine and spice – or the twentieth century's ocean liners, floating pleasure-cities for the rich. Yet even these changes were recent and superficial in terms of the global time span during which these islands emerged, when a

series of immense earth movements, protracted over millions of years, caused land to form from sedimentary deposits on the floors of oceans which then heaved out of the sea and were exposed to weathering, or were interleaved with layers of molten igneous rock. The last major event in this sequence was the massive earth-folding that uplifted the Alps and left England still attached to the Continent. Over the millennia that followed, our primitive forebears first occupied the land. During the Ice Ages which covered all but some of the southernmost parts of England, today's landscape was scoured out by glaciers and planed by ice sheets, and its present outline roughly corresponds with that of the island which was cut off from the Continent by the melting of the last ice.

Adventure in Plymouth Sound at Drake's Island. The island has served as fortress and prison but now, more appropriately, is the site of an adventure centre which offers courses in climbing, marine biology, expedition work and sailing.

1 *Invasions*

Dover's medieval castle looks down on bright lights of the twentieth century along the nineteenth-century Waterloo Crescent.

When the flooding of the English Channel created the south coast of England it also created England itself – 'this precious stone set in the silver sea' – a desirable island that could be defended once it had been overwhelmed, whose enticing white cliffs were visible from the coast of France. Celtic, Roman, Germanic, Scandinavian and Norman invaders were enticed, and have left their mark, and all along the coast traces of these successive cultures show how each one participated in the natural process of building, abandoning, submitting, and rebuilding. On the high Dorset downs that follow the Chesil bank from Abbotsbury to Bridport one can see Saxon cultivation strips superimposed on rectangular Celtic fields, while at Cissbury Hill four miles north of Worthing, a huge Iron-Age fort commanding the coast and downs has been built over Neolithic flint mines, and later taken over by the occupying Romans or used as a Romano-

British shrine. From the very beginning, the Channel waters have created not only a barrier but a bridge between England and the Continent, and Europeans have invaded these shores as much with goods, skills and ideas as with the machinery of war. Friendly or hostile, some have stayed to become part of England's complex heritage and they in turn have received settlers, missionaries or refugees, and have traded or raided across the water – sometimes sending great invasion fleets, like Edward III's to the Battle of Crecy, or Henry V's to Agincourt. At times of threat, as in Henry VIII's assertive reign or during the Napoleonic wars, castles and towers have been contructed and existing structures fortified from one end of the Channel to the other. But the real defences have been the men themselves, whose expert seamanship and shipbuilding skills have spanned the centuries preceding this leisured age of glass-reinforced plastic pleasure yachts from further back than the days of the Celtic coracle and of King Alfred's specially-built ships which he designed to repulse continuing raids from Scandinavian pirates. Alfred's ships appear in the *Anglo-Saxon Chronicle*: 'almost

twice as long as the others, some had sixty oars, some more; they were both swifter, steadier and with more freeboard'. Later in that year, AD 896, the raiders were routed off the Isle of Wight – 'so sorely crippled that they were unable to row past Sussex'.

In early times most hostile invasions took the form of piratical raids and harrassment rather than the arrival of organised forces intent on domination. The two exceptions – or rather, the exceptions that succeeded, the Roman and Norman landings – took place up-Channel, where the sea crossing was short. Both made a lasting impact on England which can be seen in buildings and cities throughout the country, but it is the ports, castles, harbours, cliffs and marshes of the Kent and East Sussex shores that perhaps remind us more than anywhere of these fateful incursions and their stirring aftermath.

The vessels of Celtic and Belgic tribes had taken shelter in natural harbours formed of deep clefts in the cliffs cut out by rivers, and this is what Julius Caesar's expeditionary force of 55 BC found when it approached Dover to find 'the enemy's forces posted on all the hills'. Caesar moved his

Lympne Castle on the edge of Romney Marsh. A fortified manor house of the fourteenth century it stands near *Portus Lemanis,* the scant remains of their seaside fort.

One of the south coast's foremost ports, Folkestone Harbour handles cross-Channel ferries, leisure boats and fishing craft.

ships on to Deal and later he reported of Dover, 'The lie of the land at this point was such that javelins could be hurled from the cliffs right on to the narrow beach enclosed between them and the sea'. One century later the conquering Romans established one of their Saxon Shore forts, *Dubris,* at this vital strategic point, but by the time the Saxons commanded the Narrow Seas, Dover's estuary was becoming choked with drifting shingle washed eastward with the tides, and the harbour had to be moved to the shelter of the western cliffs. But Dover, only 23 miles from France, proved too important strategically and too useful as a passenger port to allow its battle against silting to be lost. Unlike other Forts of the Saxon Shore at Lympne on the Romney Marsh and Pevensey in East Sussex, and unlike the Cinque Ports which grew to power in the first stirring centuries after the Norman administration, Dover's harbour has retained its

importance and Dover itself has continued to provide the same services as a port of entry and a garrison town since the Iron Age. She is the gateway to England and protector of our Channel shores, and she holds a special place in the affections of the English, for her history mirrors that of all the south coast and even of England.

The first view of Britain for thousands of Continental visitors is of the town dwarfed at the foot of massive chalk cliffs, the motorway snaking down the eastern slope to Georgian terraces beside the ferry terminal, office blocks and shops occupying the rise behind the seafront hotels, and Dover castle commanding the eastern cliffs, facing across the Straits to France. The Roman fort, *Dubris,* is covered by the modern town, and the Iron-Age and Saxon fortifications known to have occupied the castle's hill have vanished, but a Roman lighthouse, or *pharos,* stands next to the castle. The church of St Mary in Castro, for which the lighthouse once served as a bell tower, is Saxon in origin and remains so in form, although it was drastically altered last century. The castle, too, has been altered by successive administrations. The Norman tower remains; the mighty keep was built by Henry II whose reputed exhortation 'Is there none will rid me of this turbulent priest?' had brought about the murder of Thomas Becket in 1170, beginning the traffic of European pilgrims through Dover and other Channel ports to Canterbury. The Town Hall in Biggin Street today incorporates remains of a pilgrim hospice, Maison Dieu Hall, founded in 1203 by Hubert de Burgh who became Constable of the Castle, and a predecessor of Dover's Wardens of the Cinque Ports.

During this period, in the reign of Henry's son John, privateering by ships of the Cinque Ports provoked hostilities between France and England, and in 1206 Henry's powerful fortress withstood siege by the Dauphin who at the invitation of discontented barons was contender for the English crown. The following year Hubert de Burgh rallied the ports' ships against an attacking French fleet, which was roundly defeated by the use of quicklime hurled from a windward position to blind the enemy and disable his ships. Meanwhile the castle was being repaired and by the beginning of Edward I's reign its outer curtain wall and towers were complete. Henry VIII strengthened the castle as part of his coastal defence system, but by the Tudor period the increased size of shipping and the silting of up-Channel ports had reduced their commercial and military importance and the castle's appearance remained largely unchanged until the nineteenth century, when Napoleon threatened invasion, and when Dover's outer towers were reduced in size for use as gun emplacements. Underground tunnels built during the Dauphin's siege were strengthened and extended – and a use found for them as air-raid shelters in the Second World War when Dover became 'Hellfire Corner', and much of its ancient centre obliterated. The castle, its Roman lighthouse and its Saxon church survived the bombardment of both world wars.

The Romans' *Dubris* has survived through the centuries because it is preserved beneath the streets of the town. Fragments have been dug up during building operations, but they can do no more than provide tantalising glimpses of what might still exist. Other Roman remains can still be seen along this part of the coast but they have

been weathered, or incorporated into later structures. The least changed, in essence, is that haunting and fertile expanse the Romney Marsh, created by the 'inning' of cliffs arched from Hythe to Hastings. Thus the pre-Roman cliffline that extended from Dover to Hastings is now broken by marshes and by the long curve of Dungeness. This is a flat shingle cape that is continuously growing, as more shingle is deposited at every tide, and is occupied by fishermen's dwellings, a power station and a lighthouse. Between Hythe and Dungeness the coastal limit of the Romney marsh is marked by the Dymchurch Wall, originally a Roman structure but now solid concrete, still fulfilling its age-old function of keeping out the sea. From the distant inland cliffs are fabulous views over the marshes – parts still grazed by their special breed of sheep – their lonely villages and their churches lost in a landscape that is atmospheric rather than attractive. Along the foot of the cliffs the Military Canal was constructed to keep out Napoleon, and at its eastern end stands Lympne (pronounced Lim) with the crumbling remains of the Roman fort *Lemanis* standing on the cliffs between the canal and the village. A fortified manor of the fourteenth century and a Norman church stand higher up, looking out over marsh and sea.

The fort and the canal are examples of coastal defence systems that date from varying periods and extend for considerable distances along the south coast, placed there at times when England seemed particularly vulnerable to invasion. *Lemanis, Dubris* and *Anderida* at Pevensey Castle, just west of Hastings, belonged to a chain of Roman forts built as defence against Saxon pirates and operating under orders of the Count of the Saxon Shore. The forts stretched from Norfolk to Hampshire. The Normans massively fortified Roman defences, largely to demonstrate their strength to the native population they had overcome. Camber Castle, on the southern edge of Dungeness, was built by Henry VIII as part of a formidable coastal defence system covering the whole of the Channel shore. From here within a century of its construction, watchers on the cliffs in 1588 would have witnessed the great Armada drifting up-Channel, with John Hawkins' small ships giving chase – and exactly one century later spectators would have watched William of Orange's fleet, ultimately unopposed, blown down-Channel on the 'Protestant wind'. The Military Canal extended from Hythe to Winchelsea, and was backed up by squat, round,

Overleaf A working resort: fishing boats on the shingle at Hythe, one of the original Cinque Ports. Hythe's older streets lie between the Royal Military Canal and the hills.

13

Cinque Ports Pottery Ltd.
THE MONASTERY
RYE

SHOWROOM
OPEN DAILY
9 A.M. — 5 P.M.

Cinque Ports Pottery Ltd.
SHOWROOM

brick-built martello towers which can still be seen in varying forms of repair, some falling down, some incorporated into amusement parks and some serving as museums in many coastal towns of Kent and East Sussex. Originally intended to repel Napoleon's landing parties, some of the towers today stand not on the coast but inland – like *Lemanis* and *Anderida*, like Camber Castle, like the once-powerful Cinque Ports of Romney, Rye and Winchelsea – finally overcome by the most powerful invading force of all, the sea.

The Cinque Ports grew up around safe anchorages along the narrower waters of the Channel, close to the coast of France. They developed into powerful centres of herring fishing, boat building, privateering and trade, and after the Conquest they formed the formal federation known as the Cinque Ports. Dover, Hythe, Romney, Hastings and Sandwich on Kent's east coast were the original five, but Rye and Winchelsea, known as the 'ancient towns', were included as they grew in strength and prominence. Throughout the early Middle Ages the federation operated under charter from successive kings to provide ships and men in return for privileges and some payment. In this way the Narrow Seas could be guarded and used as a link between Crown properties on both sides of the Channel, and the king could rely on a fixed quota of ships – each with 21 men and a boy – for defence or for privateering, or for service in the king's campaigns, such as Edward I's against Wales. At the height of their power the Barons of the Cinque Ports followed their own rules, executed their own grim punishments and bestrode the Channel as masters. Their ships battled with the French, and the long practice of piracy and privateering was established, during which our shipwrights and seamen developed their fighting ships and tactics in seamanship at the expense of our coastal towns. Continually pillaged and burned, the seaports sent out their ships on raids and counter-raids; but still trade flourished, and the merchant ships went out prepared to defend themselves against rivals from France, Spain or Portugal – or to capture their laden ships as prizes.

Not one of the Cinque Ports – not even Dover – escaped the natural shaping process (helped by 'inning' and ballast dumping) that has been altering the south coast's shores since first the Channel was formed. From the fourteenth or fifteenth centuries, the ports' harbours grew shallower as the size of ships increased. By the mid-fifteenth century, only Dover retained any importance – the rest were marooned inland, or struggling along as fishing and boat-building towns. So they remain; and the leisure age has built new towns, with seafronts and hotels, over the original harbours and waterfronts. Hythe's Military Canal has been planted with pleasant gardens, and a martello tower on the front has been converted into a house. The picturesque old town is set back on its cliffs, crowned by Hythe's glorious church which was enlarged during the port's heyday in the thirteenth century, and has a mysterious collection of skulls and thigh bones stacked neatly in its crypt. But it is the inland ports which most successfully retain a sense of their past, for their separation from the sea has preserved them from transmogrification – tawdry or magnificent – at the hands of seaside developers. Of these the most complete is Rye, caught in all its medieval splendour, clinging to its conical hill which rises from saltings reaching out for the sea. Crowned by the spire of its twelfth-century church, its cobbled streets climbing between a profusion of gables, oriels and tiled façades, Rye is a pure and delightful example of an ancient town. Its beautifully preserved houses date from the Middle Ages to the seventeenth century, and many reflect the working skills of Flemish or Huguenot refugees. The medieval crypts and cellars were probably used for wool smuggling, practised here and in Winchelsea, when Sandwich was the only Cinque Port that had a legitimate outlet for the wool trade. Later, in the seventeenth and eighteenth centuries, local smugglers used Rye's medieval cellars as hiding places for brandy, tobacco and lace, and made their rendezvous at places like the Mermaid Inn in the steep, cobbled and romantic Mermaid Street.

Rye is a town of good views, and one of the best is from the thirteenth-century clifftop fort, the Ypres Tower, now used as a museum. From here one can see boatyards and factories and a small iron foundry clustered along the banks of Rye's still-navigable river where the masts of small sailing boats give a sense of the sea. The river ambles across the pastures for a mile or two to Rye Harbour – and then, for another mile, to the coast. The tower, and Rye's handsome Land Gate, once formed part of the walled town, and they survive from a French raid of 1377 which burned Rye to the ground. The raiders carried off, with other booty, the church bells. Some parts of the twelfth-century church still stand, but work

The ancient streets of Rye cling to its conical hill, once lapped by the sea. This Cinque Port of medieval days still has boat yards along the banks of the River Rother, and a number of fishing craft.

The fourteenth-century gatehouse of Battle Abbey, all that remains of William I's symbol of ecclesiastic power.

from varying periods contributes to the whole. The church clock with its Quarterboys (one a girl) is said to be the oldest working tower clock in England, and was made in the 1560s by a Winchelsea craftsman. It was the men of Winchelsea who, two centuries earlier, had recovered Rye's stolen bells in an equally-ferocious reprisal raid on the French coastal towns. Winchelsea was one of the most formidable and powerful of the Cinque Ports. It was Edward I who planned the present town after the old town had been almost completely destroyed by a storm in which, an early writer tells us, 'the moon, upon her change, appeared exceeding red and swelled' and the sea 'forced contrarie to his natural course, flowed twice without ebbing, yielding such a rooring that the same was heard (not without great wonder), a farre distance from the shore'. Winchelsea

suffered widespread devastation, including '300 houses and some churches drowned', and some years later when the new town was already established a few miles distant, an even worse storm washed old Winchelsea away. The new town flourished, but within a century was suffering encroachment of the land – not so dramatic, more gradual, but no less effective in reducing this boisterous Cinque Port to a quiet town standing on a cliff plateau with a view of the sea across a coastal plain. So we see it now, approached through substantial medieval gateways which open on to residential streets of period houses with no particular focus other than the cathedral-like church dedicated to Thomas Becket which occupies one of the eight squares envisaged by Edward I. Neither church nor town was ever completed, for Winchelsea and Rye ultimately shared the same fate, and today they

stand looking toward the distant shore, land-locked and time-locked – beautiful relics, preserved by their own decline.

West of Winchelsea, past Camber Castle and the watery Pett Level haunted by waterfowl and swans, a sandstone ridge protruding between the North and South Downs forms a range of sea cliffs that reaches from here to Hastings. At Fairlight Cove the great walls of sandstone rising sheer from the beach are topped by seaside villas and bungalows set amid clifftop gardens of tamarisk, laurel, red-hot-poker and pampas, with a narrow by-road snaking up and down between. They make a pleasant contrast to the wild beauties of the westward cliffs, burning with gorse in the summer, riven with overgrown gullies and their splashing streams; a stretch of wilderness with sweeping views from Dungeness to Beachy Head that makes an exhilarating approach to an

exciting town. It was to Hastings' cliffs that William of Normandy turned after arriving further down-Channel to be faced with the inhospitable terrain of Pevensey's wealden hinterland where six centuries earlier, as the *Anglo-Saxon Chronical* relates, 'Aelle and Cissa besieged *Andredescester* and slew all the inhabitants; there was not even one Briton left there'. A medieval fortress enclosed in its Roman walls, Pevensey Castle today stands at the edge of the beautiful Pevensey Levels and overlooks the untidy development of the shore; but in those harsh

Cinque Port, fishing town and seaside resort: Hastings with its historic associations and sea breezes really can offer 'something for everyone'.

19

times its desolate surroundings drove William's fleet with his infantry, his cavalry and his prefabricated wooden castle eastward – and in so doing created at Hastings one of England's most important historic sites.

Hastings was the principal Cinque Port of Sussex and for a time the most powerful of them all, and like its neighbours it suffered sacking from French raiding parties and devastation from storms only to become wedged in by the ceaseless build-up of pebbles that finally rendered it useless as a seaport. Today it enjoys the combined roles of celebrated site, ancient sea town and traditional south coast resort. An impressive conglomeration of seaside and vernacular architecture ranges over cliff and shore, presided over by the Norman castle, half-vanished over the cliff edge. In the old town – an indispensable concomitant of the new – a steep and narrow street of ancient buildings tilts down to the eastward end of the promenade and to the fishermen's beach where nets are stored in the elongated, narrow lofts called net shops, weatherboarded and tarred, that first appeared at Hastings in Elizabethan times. The wooden fishing boats, loosely modelled on the original Hastings Luggers, are winched over the shingle to

shelter under the looming sandstone cliff known as the Rock-a-Nore. Here the East Hill Lift, a product of Victorian railway technology, leads straight up the cliff face from a solid brick kiosk advertising 'Glorious views and walks'. Westward in the modern town an energetic sequence of seaside building from all periods overlies the ancient harbour which was held between the cliffs of East and West Hill. Most arresting is Pelham Crescent, built in 1824, which has as its centrepiece a small, white, Grecian-looking church flanked by the sweeping terraces of grey houses and surmounted by wild-looking sandstone cliffs. In the Town Hall is the Hastings Embroidery which was made to commemorate the 900th anniversary of the Battle of Hastings – fought on a hillside six miles inland.

The market town of Battle stands there now, deep in the Sussex countryside, its old unchanging High Street sloping up to the great gatehouse of the ruined abbey that the Conqueror built on the site where Harold fell. Battle is much visited but it lacks the diversions of the seaside, so the crowds arrive, marvel, and depart – to seek the salty excitements of clifftops, shingle, piers and promenades in the seaside resorts.

Nestling under Hastings' eastern cliffs are the distinctive net shops and the boats of the old fishing town.

2 Brighton Rock &
Sea Breezes

The old-world charm of places like Battle or Rye has been preserved through remoteness from the sea, but some of the south coast's most striking architecture is so because it stands 'beside the seaside' and still fulfills the purpose for which it was planned. The craze among the leisured classes for seeking health from seaside spas took hold late in the eighteenth century, at a time when Georgian architects were expressing their ideas in graceful compositions which integrated their beautifully-proportioned buildings into sweeping crescents, or grouped them around spacious squares. The small fishing towns whose sea and breezes were suddenly in such demand provided all the space required for set-pieces which reflected their spectacular location near majestic headlands or spreading cliffs, often dazzling white, caught between sea and sky. Regency designs followed with creamy stucco façades, bay windows and lacy verandas that reflected the notion – encouraged by the Prince Regent – that health-seeking could be fun. Perhaps the most felicitous development came with the Victorians, for although their insensitive improvements spoiled many of our ancient churches, here at the seaside they let their hair down and used their new technology to produce structures with a unique combination of delicacy and strength. Long slender piers, pavilions of cast-iron and glass and riotous tracery in ironwork ornamentation show a voluptuous appreciation of existing composition, and of the breath-taking views beyond.

The spa town of Scarborough in Yorkshire was the first seaside place to be developed as a resort, early in the eighteenth century, but the south coast was quick to follow with the jewel of resorts, Brighton, and a succession of gems that

vulgarly glittered or refinedly glowed, from Folkestone in Kent to Torquay in Devon. So they glow or glitter still, treasuries of Georgian and Regency architecture embellished with the Victorians' ironwork and their formal gardens full of rockeries, gazebos, exotic shrubs and dark evergreens. The twentieth century has made its contribution in places like Bognor, with its fine *art nouveau* shopping arcade and its Picturedrome – still a cinema – facing the Victorian railway station. The De la Warr Pavilion in Bexhill on Sea was ambitiously designed in the 1930s by Mendelsohn and Chermayeff, while at Hastings the Italianate White Rock Pavilion from that period still functions as an entertainment centre, and at St Leonard's, further along the Promenade, the Marina Court intrudes on James Burton's stately Royal Victoria Hotel, started in 1828. Big, bold and bulbous, Marina Court has been declared a tasteless interruption of Burton's sequence of pediments and columns; yet both share a sense of time and style, and both share qualities characteristic of seaside architecture – one refinedly elegant, the other brash.

The seaside architecture of Hastings and its westward extension, St Leonard's, has been integrated with an older town of some standing which already held a place in history and had a distinction of its own. But the places that epitomise the popular idea of the resort, refined or brash, are those in 'Sussex by the Sea' – Eastbourne, Brighton, Worthing and Bognor Regis – perhaps because they are purpose-built

Sussex by the Sea at Eastbourne's sea front. This handsome resort is said to enjoy more sunshine than almost any other town in Britain.

for pleasure, and seem to have the greatest concentration of all that is best in seaside architecture. Eastbourne is by far the most elegant. Seventeen miles from Hastings, it was laid out in 1834 by the seventh Duke of Devonshire at a point where the coast again begins to rise into dramatic cliff scenery. The Duke's graceful series of terraces, tree-lined streets and formal gardens integrated the old fishing town, then a mile inland, with the speculative seafront development that preceded the new resort. Today Eastbourne is famous for its parks, and for the Carpet Gardens whose flower beds along the front make vivid contrast with the handsome cliff-like terraces of Grand Parade. Another feature of the Grand Parade is the Victorian bandstand with its roof of brilliant blue tiles, redolent of a flying saucer, supported by Grecian-style columns – a fine fusion of the Classic and the futuristic, set in a sunken colonnaded court where from striped deckchairs holidaymakers can soak up the sun and listen to the band. Beyond, reaching out across the waves, Eastbourne's magnificent pier and pavilion hover like a mirage. All this, of course, in good weather

– but Eastbourne is noted, also, for its record as one of the sunniest spots in Britain. At the eastward end of the town, where the fishing boats are, a formidable Napoleonic fortress, the Redoubt, stands near the Leisure Pool and holds an intriguing display of our historical defence systems. There is an equally fascinating display in the martello tower on the front, the Wish Tower, and nearby – perhaps most important of all – is the first-ever museum of the Royal National Lifeboat Institution. From the Wish Tower one sees the sweep of the seafront, flowerbeds and the pier, with the coast vanishing towards Hastings; and to the west across the water is the distant, rearing mass of Beachy Head – scene of past sea battles and shipwrecks, grand finale of the South Downs – and Eastbourne's greatest attribute.

Writing on Sussex in the 1830s, J D Parry described this massive headland, rising more than 500 feet above the sea, as 'one of the finest marine eminences in Europe'. There is a red-and-white striped lighthouse dwarfed at its foot, built in 1902 to replace the Belle Tout light further along the cliff top, which used to get obscured by

Opposite Beachy Head lighthouse dwarfed by the south coast's highest headland – 534 feet of chalk cliff. The light from the lighthouse, flashing twice every 20 seconds, is visible for 16 miles.

Castle on the Arun: for centuries the seat of the Earls of Arundel, this magnificent fortress was largely rebuilt in the eighteenth century. Traces of the Norman buildings remain.

cloud. Hidden from the top of the cliff is an earlier, primitive lighthouse – a cave excavated in the eighteenth century by a local parson, who would hang a lantern in its mouth as a warning to ships. Local gossip had it that the cave served also as a retreat from a nagging wife. The long stretch of cliffs reaching from here to Seaford also served bands of smugglers in those times, particularly at points where the cliffs are breached – the Birling Gap, and the beautiful Cuckmere Haven. A lonely coastal path follows these cliffs over chalky downland turf, echoing with the sound of waves and the incessant song of larks – or lashed by icy wind and reverberating with the thunder of the mighty sea – while the incomparable prospect of the Seven Sisters cliffs ranging graceful and dramatic along the western coastline appears at vantage points in all the seaside suburbs, old seaports, busy dockyards and fabulous Regency promenades along the built-up West Sussex coast.

The rise of the seaside resorts was encouraged by royal patronage to which each up-and-coming town aspired, and for which sleepy fishing villages were decked in Terraces and Crescents,

or old seaports like Weymouth were endowed with Georgian Esplanades. Although Brighton was, and remains, the Queen of resorts, it was far-westward Weymouth, sheltering in the lee of Portland, which first received a royal visit. In 1789 George III came here, and was much astonished when the band struck up 'God Save the King' as his bathing machine first ventured forth into the waves. The King sent his daughter Amelia to Worthing to recover from an unfortunate love affair, and her sister Charlotte brought popularity to Bognor, later revived when George V convalesced here for a period and granted the title 'Regis' to the town whose centre today has a spirited blend of Regency, Victorian and Edwardian styles. Some Georgian examples remain from the first entrepreneurial days, notably Dome House in Bognor Road, and Spencer Terrace, while the delightful flower-decked Regency sequences of Heene Terrace or Ambrose Place add to the pleasures of Worthing – whose imaginatively-designed public gardens rival anything on the south coast. Both Worthing and Bognor were developed in the wake of the south coast's most dazzling success story: the rise

Messing about at Newhaven: situated at the mouth of the River Ouse, this pleasant and unpretentious cross-Channel port also caters for holiday yachts.

Opposite White cliffs at Peacehaven, East Sussex. A mile or so inland are the rolling contours of the beautiful South Downs.

27

of Brighthelmstone, a fishing town fallen on hard times (Defoe in 1719 wrote of 'above one hundred houses having been devoured by water in a few years past'), to fame and fortune as Brighton – favoured residence of George III's son the Prince of Wales, later to become Prince Regent. The town had been promoted by Dr Richard Russell of Lewes as a health spa, and the nobility had flocked here to take the waters, but the Prince and Mrs Fitzherbert soon dispensed with this idea, and came here to enjoy themselves. Henry Holland started his classical Royal Pavilion in 1787, and in 1815 John Nash began to transform the exterior into an eye-catching and exotic residence – just as Brighton had been transformed by Prinny, Mrs Fitzherbert and their circle into a spacious and handsome town. So it remains, unfolding along a broad sea front that opens on a sequence of squares and colonnaded crescents beyond which can be seen the rolling Sussex Downs; and so it merges imperceptibly with its neighbour Hove. Nash's outlandish masterpiece once enjoyed an uninterrupted sea view, but now it sits hedged in with buildings at the far end of Old Steine, a large open space busy with traffic where the Pavilion's domes, oriental arches and trellis-work verandas can be seen across lawns and flowerbeds. The sumptuous and extravagant *Chinoiserie* within – the painted columns, the Chinese murals, the amazing domed ceiling of the banqueting hall and its gigantic chandelier held in a silver dragon's claw, even the motifs of palm and other exotica that extend to the kitchens – has to be seen to be believed.

Brighton with its Pavilion quickly became the archetypal south coast resort, to be emulated and rivalled all along the coast. The south coast became increasingly popular as the Napoleonic wars based naval families at Portsmouth, Portland and Torbay, and turned the attentions of the leisured classes from Biarritz to Brighton and points east or west. Fifty years later the opening of the railways boosted many would-be resorts into fashionable holiday towns, opening fresh avenues for developers (among them the railway companies themselves), creating the need for family hotels, and giving rein to some wonderfully grandiose designs. The new construction techniques were expressed in cliff

Sun and sea breezes along the prom, characterised by Brighton's Victorian piers. The Palace Pier, in the foreground, is one-third of a mile long.

Opposite Brighton's Royal Pavilion, built for the Prince Regent – later George IV – in the late eighteenth century. The Pavilion once attracted criticism for its extravagant style.

lifts, funicular railways or dizzying landscaped
promenades, like the Leas at Folkestone, that
gave wide views from above or descended
precipitously through formal shrubberies to the
beach. At every stage Brighton kept pace, setting
standards that were followed up and down the
coast, so that today the south's resorts owe much
to this 'most celebrated' of seaside towns.

The arbours, architecture and appurtenances
of the south coast's seaside towns occupy a
special corner in the mosaic of English building
styles. Although the towns vary according to their
history and their siting along cliff or strand, each
follows the charming and obligatory formula of
the resort: the pier, the pavilion, the promenade.
But the views extending beyond the piers cannot
conform, for together they reflect all the rich
diversity of the English landscape. An excursion
westward out of Eastbourne brings the visitor
onto the blowy chalk cliffs of the South Downs,
while the coast ranging east of Lyme Regis could
only belong to Dorset. Beyond the dark, fossil-
rich height of Black Ven with Charmouth and its
High Street of thatched houses nestling just
above the beach is a wild and isolated stretch of

inaccessible coves whose cliff tops have been
planted by smugglers with clumps of trees for
landmarks. Further east the crescent bay of
Chideock lies in the arm of sandstone cliffs
topped with turf and sheltered by the proud
eminence of Golden Cap, at 617 feet the highest
cliff on the south coast. Chideock's thatched
cottages are built of this pale golden stone. The
Sussex resorts may exemplify the inimitable
flavours of the pleasure town, but the beautiful
surroundings of the holiday places all along the
coast add an extra dimension belonging to that
place alone.

On the sheltered east coast of the scenic Isle of
Wight the seaside resorts of Ryde, Sandown,
Shanklin and Ventnor all grew up in Victoria's
time, for it was in the northern part of the island
that she and Albert as young-marrieds built
Osborne House – designed by the Prince Consort
and the developer Thomas Cubitt in the
Italianate style – and it was here that the Queen
came as a young widow to grieve, and as an old
woman to die. The island's varied scenery and
sense of other-worldliness appealed to her
subjects as they appealed to the Queen, for here

was an enchanting island of windswept downs, undulating fields, stone and thatch cottages, manor houses, ancient churches and mills, all encompassed in 60 miles of coastline with its own contrasts, from the breathtaking sweep of Sandown Bay to the saltings and mud flats of the west coast's river estuaries, the grassy heights of Tennyson Down, or the fantastic aspect of the chines – ravine-like fissures in the cliffs tangled with undergrowth and trees through which rivers tumble to the sea. The developers busied themselves with providing for the holiday crowds and the inevitable invalids, and Ryde's long sandy beach was bordered with its Esplanade, while Sandown's new pier stretched out almost 1000 feet into Sandown Bay. At Shanklin a path was excavated along the banks of the stream rippling between the romantic, ferny, and plunging woodlands of Shanklin Chine. Ventnor under its tall cliffs grew upward rapidly and haphazardly, and today its steep terraces of buildings have a Mediterranean look. With its balmy air that allows the growth of cork trees, myrtle and palm, sleepy Ventnor awoke to become 'England's Positano', attracting the

sophisticated sickly encouraged by the physician Sir James Clark who recommended the mild atmosphere of Ventnor and the Undercliff as a relief for sufferers of respiratory complaints. The four miles of wild, overgrown slopes sprawling from Ventnor to the island's southernmost tip, which form the fantastic scenery of the Undercliff, would make a rewarding excursion for anyone – chesty or healthy.

To Tennyson who had a residence on the western edge of the island the fresh air of the downs was 'worth sixpence a pint', but the languid breezes of places like Ventnor, Bournemouth or Torquay were worth more to Victorian developers.

In the growing resort of Bournemouth they planted the Invalids' Walk, an avenue of pines, Veronica and Rhododendron, where invalids could be wheeled in their carriages to inhale the 'balsamic effluvia' – pine-scented air. Bournemouth today is a leading retirement and holiday centre, but less than two centuries ago this was desolate heathland, uncultivable, stretching westward from the New Forest toward the Dorset heaths. The high cliffs, gashed by

All the fun of the fair at Shanklin, one of the Isle of Wight's popular east coast resorts.

Overleaf Island magic: the cliffs at Freshwater on the Isle of Wight's western coast. Tennyson, who made his home here in 1853, trod these paths.

31

The Needles, eroded chalk pinnacles that once formed a ridge of chalk hills linking the Isle of Wight to the far-off Dorset coast.

chines, were overrun by smugglers' bands who operated all along the shores of Bournemouth Bay from Hengistbury Head to Poole Harbour – much of which is now infilled with immaculate suburbs. In the mid-nineteenth century, on these wild south-facing cliffs, a seaside village was laid out and pine trees planted, and so Bournemouth began. Although these shallow-rooted trees do not readily take root in this sandy soil, by 1890 there were 3000 pines of varying varieties – Scots, Austrian, Monterey and Maritime – and Bournemouth's motto was born: *Pulchritudo et Salubritas,* meaning 'Beauty and Salubrity'. Later the town set out to maintain an air of refinement by various stratagems, among them the banning of donkeys from the beach – and, on a higher plane, the creation of the Bournemouth Symphony Orchestra. Refinement, orchestra, pines and chines are still features of this handsome Victorian and twentieth-century town, although the recent adoption by the Tourist Board of the theme 'Never a Dull Moment' shows Bournemouth's more progressive aspirations.

Refinement and pines are features of the rich suburbs that follow the coastline around Bournemouth, and these seaside villas in their luxuriant shrubberies make their own agreeable contribution to the traveller's task of finding the way to the sea, or to town. For a resort with an untamed setting Lyme Regis would be hard to beat, and in its position on the Dorset border with Devon it has some of the wildest and strangest cliff scenery along the south coast. The dark clays and shales of the cliffs, alternating with layers of limestone, are rich in ammonites and have yielded some important finds. Most notable was that of Mary Anning, who as a child in 1811 came across a 21-foot fossilised ichthyosaurus at Black Ven, just east of the town. Lyme made an appropriate setting for the film *The French Lieutenant's Woman* from John Fowles' novel, whose hero had an interest in palaeontology – but its wild environs, steep streets and rushing stream, and its much-rebuilt sea wall, the Cobb, provide a fine setting even without the added fascination for fossil hunters. Jane Austen lived here for a time, when Lyme was finding its feet as a resort, and she featured the Cobb in her novel *Persuasion.* But by then Lyme already had an ancient history, for it was never a purpose-built

resort, and is known to have been a Saxon salt-panning town, a medieval cloth port, and later to have been an important town in the Newfoundland fisheries trade. Edward I granted Lyme its charter, giving it the title *Regis* and encouraging the building of the Cobb – which helped cause the silting and decline of the harbour in later centuries. It was outside this harbour that Drake first encountered the great ships of the Spanish Armada, and it was here that the ill-equipped, ill-fated and illegitimate Duke of Monmouth landed in 1685, hoping to displace the pro-Catholic James II from the throne and inspiring the rhyme

> Lyme, though but a little town,
> I think it wonderous pretty;
> And if I come to wear the crown
> I'll make of it a city.

To the west of this pretty town, between here and Beer Head in Devon, lies the wild and dangerous cliffline of the Great Landslip of 1839, its botanic peculiarities graphically portrayed in Fowles' novel: '. . . its wild arbutus and ilex and other trees rarely seen growing in England; its enormous

ashes and beeches; its green Brazilian chasms choked with ivy and the liana of wild clematis. . . . In summer it is the nearest this country can offer to a tropical jungle'. Or, as the author quotes from Jane Austen's *Persuasion*: '. . . a scene so wonderful and so lovely is exhibited, as may more than equal any of the resembling scenes of the far-famed Isle of Wight. . . .'

This rare landscape makes an appropriate opening – or finale – to the vivid and geologically-complex coastline of South Devon. At Seaton Bay the cliffs turn all chalk-white, and from Beer Head to Babbacombe Bay, far beyond the Exmouth and Teignmouth estuaries, the dominant colour of the rock is red – sometimes pinkish and bright, sometimes, as around Dawlish, jagged terracotta. In many places the fields and woods reach to the cliff edge, and the shoreline belongs as much to rural as to coastal Devon. At Sidmouth, sheer Red Sandstone cliffs rear up along the shore, while the town's Regency terraces and fanciful 'cottage orné' villas are embraced by the wooded valley of the river Sid. Queen Victoria was brought here as an infant, and her father died here of a cold; the Grand

Soaking up the sun at Bournemouth. Developed as a health resort in the nineteenth century, the town today flourishes as a holiday and retirement centre.

Fishing boats at Lyme Regis, a town famous for its fossils. Jane Austen favoured it as a watering place.

Opposite Traditional seaside fare at Lyme. The town was granted its first Charter by Edward I in 1284, and for many centuries was one of England's foremost trading ports.

Duchess of Russia settled at a villa in Fortfield Terrace. One wonders whether the Duchess would have appreciated Sidmouth in the same way as a twentieth-century visitor, Sir John Betjeman: 'Ah! to bathe as I did in warm summer water, and swim towards the great pink cliffs and creamy stucco esplanade!' – or as the enthusiasts who come for the Sidmouth Folk Song Festival every summer. Earlier this century the encroachment of then-modern building dismayed Charles Harper who in his book on the south Devon coast scolded, 'Why, confound the purblind, bat like stupidity of it! red brick is not wanted at Sidmouth, where the cliffs are the very reddest of all Devon....' The writer goes on to extol Sidmouth's 'terraces and isolated squares of cool, contrasting whiteness', and gives short shrift to its rival Torquay's buildings, 'painted in wholly immoral shades of drab and dun, green, pink, and red'.

These 'immoral shades' and others are shown in the extraordinarily varying sequence of cliff and rock scenery around the coast between Torquay and Babbacombe (Gerard Manley Hopkins' 'red cliffs, white ashy shingle, green

inshore water, blue above that' remain unaltered), for the exposed rocks change from New Red Sandstone at Oddicombe Bay to limestone, or slate and sandstone, and at Black Head to a dark igneous rock called Dolerite. The cliff path follows the popular 'Bishop's Walk' from the limestone crags of Anstey's Cove across Black Head and along a curve of slate cliff to the limestone headland, Hope's Nose. Near here is one of Torquay's handsome hotels, built in the nineteenth century as a palace for the Bishop of Exeter. Near here also Kent's Cavern, a remarkable series of limestone caves, was discovered in 1824 and excavated in 1880, when under varying layers of limestone were found human bones and flint tools together with bones of bear, bison, rhinoceros, mammoth and other un-English beasts. The caves can be toured, and the once-controversial remains seen in Torquay's Natural History Museum. When first discovered, the presence of human bones aroused the sensibilities of those who believed that Adam and Eve had been created at a later date than was demonstrated by the positioning of the remains beneath the sedimentary rock. It was around this

time that Hesketh Crescent was built just south at Meadowfoot Bay, which looks across at slatey, dark rocks clustered with seabirds – Thatcher Rock and the Ore Stone and Shag Rock. The curve of residential villas, emulating the architecture of Bath, is now the Osborne Hotel and enveloped in the outskirts of Torquay. Set in this checkerboard of cliff and rock, suburbs and hills, Torquay today has the feel of a southern town, still with some Georgian and Victorian villas climbing the hills around the spacious harbour, and a good many modern blocks between. The Terrace, a street of Captains' houses of the early 1900s, gives an idea of the town before it was developed by the Palk family for naval people based at Torbay, when its warm winters and lush vegetation gave it the status of a spa. For much of the present century, it has become the traditional glamour spot for honeymooners from the South-West Peninsula, and its palms, luxury hotels, floodlit terraced gardens and scenic Marine Drive give it a suitably

romantic atmosphere on balmy summer nights. Some of the oldest buildings are at Torre Abbey, where an eleventh-century tithe barn and a fourteenth-century gatehouse survive from the original Norman abbey, and a predominantly eighteenth-century house contains Torquay's Art Gallery and Museum. Nearby is the Princess Theatre, built in 1961.

Large and metropolitan, Torquay's past belongs more to our social history than in the annals of momentous national events. One occasion is worth recording, for it involved the *bête-noire* of the British, the fearful 'Boney' whose belligerent attitudes, ironically, played such a part in the establishment of Torquay and other pleasure towns. After his surrender in 1815 Napoleon was brought on the *HMS Bellerophon* to Torbay, as Charles Harper describes, 'to be revealed to the gaping hundreds who put off in boats to see him, as merely a little fat man, clean-shaven, melancholy, and obviously unwell,

mildly pacing the quarter-deck, and saying unexpectedly complimentary things about the scenery and the climate'. Only a few years before Napoleon's rise to power, when the French Revolution was at its height, a Brighton newspaper for 29 August 1792 gave an illuminating account of the social round in this fashionable resort:

The Marchioness de Beaule is arrived at this place, in an open boat, for which she paid two hundred guineas at Dieppe...she was under necessity of appearing in the uniform of a sailor, and as such assisted the men...in order to bring with her undiscovered a favoured female, whom it is confidently said, she conveyed on board in a trunk. ... The marchioness was received, on coming on shore, by his highness the Prince of Wales, with Mrs Fitzherbert and Miss Isabella Pigot. The prince, with his usual affability, escorted the fair fugitive to Earl Clermont's, where tea was provided for the prince and twenty of his friends.

Lights over the water: a soft summer's evening in Torquay.

Opposite Harbour and gardens at Torquay, one resort of many that grew at the time of the Napoleonic wars.

3 Great Ships &
Sequestered Shores

Through the ages, the mariners and shore dwellers of the south coast have learnt seamanship and shipbuilding skills on every type of craft from the Celtic coracle to the container ship. In the present century, age-old skills continue hand in hand with modern techniques while the most advanced craft share the Channel waters with traditional fishing boats and leisure yachts or sailing dinghies. Every small haven from Rye to Salcombe has its boatyard turning out fishing and pleasure boats in glass-reinforced plastic or steel or, as for thousands of years, in wood. Fishermen put out in clinker-built boats based on the design of the original Hastings Lugger and showing the same rounded but graceful line, and you can still see original Chesil Lerrets hauled over the shingle of the 'Steepstone Bank'. Great liners and massive container ships sail from Southampton, one of the world's leading passenger and cargo ports, situated at the head of the deep, drowned river valley Southampton Water. Pleasure launches ply from Southampton's Royal Pier and Town Quay; coasting vessels put in at smaller berths and wharves all along the river Itchen, and in the season the waters of the Hamble and Beaulieu rivers are teeming with yachts of all colours and sizes, while the international events of 'Cowes Week' culminating in the highly-prized Admiral's Cup series still satisfy the highest aspirations of world class yachtsmen.

Since medieval times the mid-Channel coast, from Littlehampton in Sussex to Lymington in Hampshire, has been a nerve-centre of Channel shipping. When shingle choked the up-Channel ports the base of England's maritime trade and power shifted to the sheltered creeks, deep waters and double tides of the coastline bordering the Hampshire basin. On the map, this region makes a sizeable but shallow indentation, with the Isle of Wight looking like the last piece of a jigsaw waiting for a cosmic finger to push it into place. The northern tip of the island's diamond shape sits opposite the mouth of Southampton Water and the Hamble River, flanked on the east by a series of lagoon-like harbours, Chichester, Langstone and Portsmouth, biting into the curve of flat land that faces Wight's north-east coast across the waters of Spithead. The land continues south-eastward to Selsey Bill, the most southerly point in Sussex, and includes the lonely fossil-rich sands of Bracklesham Bay – an unspoiled stretch of Selsey's shores. To the west of Southampton Water, facing the Isle of Wight's marshy north-western coast, the heathy slopes of the New Forest reach toward the Solent waters, and are breached by the estuaries of the Beaulieu and Lymington rivers. Beyond, the long curve of the coast ranges eastward to Poole Harbour and the east-facing coast of Purbeck.

Poole Harbour and the waters of the Hampshire basin benefit from a freak two tides a day caused by the flow of tides up-Channel meeting the down-Channel tide from the North Sea. For centuries the waters of Chichester Harbour and the Solent, with their wealth of sheltered inlets and the deep arm of Southampton Water screened by the Isle of Wight, have produced or harboured some of England's greatest ships – among them the three-masted trading vessels developed in the fifteenth century, the formidable fighting ships of Henry VIII's navy, and great men-of-war like Nelson's flagship *Agamemnon*, built on the forested banks of the Beaulieu River. Meanwhile the fertile land between the South Downs and the coast has been cultivated, cathedrals and palaces and castles built, history played out with its roots in the land as well as the water; and the land banked up or eaten away by the restless and indifferent sea.

Just to the east of Selsey is the jolly yachting town of Littlehampton, also a working port, with boatyards, busy docks which export timber and stone, and some fine old houses on the waterfront. The town stands at the mouth of the Arun between Worthing and Bognor, and it combines business with pleasure by providing swathes of sandy beaches and two small yachting marinas beyond its swing bridge. Further up-river is beautiful Arundel, for which Littlehampton was once merely the out-port. Masts and spas of small yachts still enliven the river from which the old town rises to its powerful castle, ancestral home of the Dukes of Norfolk. The castle was begun soon after the Conquest and magnificently rebuilt in the eighteenth and nineteenth centuries, and today Arundel has the flavour of a country town rather than of a busy port. Yet there was a flourishing timber and shipbuilding industry here in the sixteenth century, and even in the 1930s Arundel's river could be described as 'the means of considerable traffic in coals and corn between London and the Mediterranean'. Situated 3½ miles inland at the foot of the wooded downs, Arundel has escaped the demands made of a seaside town – and the river in its meadows, the half-timbered houses across the bridge, the old steep High Street, the Victorian-Gothic Roman Catholic cathedral and the hilltop castle retain their dignity unimpaired.

Ironically, all this curving shoreline from Beachy Head to Selsey Bill has suffered not only abandonment but encroachment by the sea. Beyond Littlehampton the coast has been so severely eroded within the last two centuries that houses, churches and even whole villages have crumbled under the waves. Some way offshore from the town of Pagham on the Selsey peninsula local legend tells of church bells sounding from beneath the waters where the Christian missionary St Wilfrid's cathedral lies, with its monastery and deer park. The cathedral stood on dry land from late in the seventh century, when Wilfrid returned to Sussex to convert the pagan Saxons, at least until after the Conquest. Soon after that, the bishopric was transferred to Chichester in the face of the advancing water. The stretch where the cathedral and its grounds are thought to lie is known by local fishermen as the Parks.

To fishermen and yachtsmen the waters of the Channel have their own topography, and the Parks, like the Bognor Rocks, the Owers Shoal and the dreaded Portland Race are known and charted for seamen's guidance just as the hikers' or motorists' maps record marshes, castles, towns. But here the flat expanses of Selsey, and of Chichester and Langstone Harbours (separated by Hayling Island), create a confusion of water and land. Pagham Harbour has alternated between tidal lagoon and pasture through successive flooding and 'inning' since Norman times; Chichester Harbour is formed by four deep indentations winding far inland and on one of these, Bosham Channel, Bosham's waterfront road appears only at low tide. The area is popular not only for yachting, but for its rich birdlife and its historical associations, which are pleasantly interlocked and often can be explored within the compass of a single village or town. Most rewarding is Chichester, that ancient city set within reach of the sea and the South Downs.

The cathedral with its fine spire stands out as a landmark across both land and sea. The spire is a handsome replica of the original, which fell down in 1861 –

> If Chichester Church steeple fall,
> In England there's no king at all

– and was replaced by Sir Gilbert Scott. It has served seafarers since it was first added in about 1300, at the same time as the cathedral's unique detached bell tower, and it rises above the Norman cathedral of a city which is named after its Saxon governor, whose Georgian streets follow the Roman layout of the city built for the accommodating king of the region's Celtic tribe whom the Romans named Cogidubnus. As the Romans' *Noviomagus* and the Saxon *Cissa's Ceaster,* Chichester was Sussex's capital and it remains the county town of West Sussex, an important agricultural centre which once ranked as one of England's major ports and which today has been compared with Bath as custodian of England's Georgian heritage. Some of the most complete and handsome Georgian buildings are to be seen in the four streets called the Pallants whose layout resembles a miniature Chichester, and which forms a section of the city that gave palatine rights to the Archbishop of Chichester in the Middle Ages. One of the finest is the red-brick Pallant House, occupied by the Chichester District Council, built by Henry Pelham in 1712. The symmetry and grace of the building is

HMS Victory, flagship of Lord Nelson at the Battle of Trafalgar, in no. 2 dock at Portsmouth. Built at Chatham and launched in 1765, she mounted 100 guns and was classed as a first-rate ship of the line.

complemented by rich plasterwork over the doorway and offset by curious-looking stone birds which adorn the gateposts and were carved as ostriches, but in fact gave the house its local name – Dodo House. Chichester is a comfortable city, for all its elegant beauty. The four main streets meet at the market cross, a large and elaborately-ornamented octagon, rising 50 feet to a long, graceful cupola and looking a little like a crown – the largest jewels being the four clocks, added in 1724, almost 250 years after the cross was built. The cathedral is sited down in the city, among its streets, rising from West Street opposite the Dolphin and Anchor, and flanked by its Georgian precincts and Roman or medieval walls to the south; meadows beyond, and the river Lavant beyond that. Inside, the austere Norman lines prevail, despite two fires in the twelfth century and depredations after the Civil War. Earlier Norman work is mainly in Quarr stone from the Isle of Wight, while pillars of Purbeck marble soar in the nave, built after the fire of 1187. Twentieth-century additions include Graham Sutherland's painting *Noli Me Tangere* and John Piper's vivid tapestry behind the altar, and in the south wall of the choir aisle are two ancient bas-reliefs representing Christ's visit to Martha and Mary, and the raising of Lazarus – possibly remnants of the drowned cathedral of Selsey.

yachtsmen and naturalists for whom the waters and the muddy fringes of Chichester Harbour provide all that the holiday heart desires.

For those interested in legends and histories Bosham's part-Saxon church, the oldest in Sussex, has its share in both. The church's tenor bell was said to have been stolen by Danish raiders whose boat could not support its holy weight, and peals ring in legend from beneath the creek – but more tangible and more touching, in the nave of the church, is the tomb of an eight-year-old girl who for some time was thought to be Canute's daughter, drowned in nearby waters. Canute lived here for a time, and today's residents claim that he made his famous command to the tides from these shores, but no written or pictorial evidence exists to support either story or siting. Harold's visit later in the same century, as he set out from Bosham for his fateful meeting with William Duke of Normandy, is depicted in the Bayeux tapestry and thus takes its place not in legend but in history. The most thrilling physical record of the past yet found among these hamlets caught between water and land, and one of the most important in Britain, can be seen in the superb and elaborate mosaic floors of a vast Roman palace unearthed near Chichester at the village of Fishbourne. The palace, which covered about six acres, is thought to have been built for Cogidubnus and was occupied from about AD 75 until late in the third century, when it was destroyed by fire. Most of it lies beneath the main road and a modern estate, but the excavated north wing, protected by a pleasant covering of wood and glass, reveals remains of walls and hypocausts as well as the outstanding craftsmanship which went into the pictorial and geometric designs of tessellated floors covering different rooms. Among the most beautiful, and perhaps reflecting Fishbourne's position before its desertion by the tides, is the motif of a boy on a dolphin which forms a centrepiece skirted by a seahorse on each side. Formal gardens on which the apartments opened have retained clear evidence of their original layout, and this has been followed faithfully in re-creation of the gardens which are planted with bushes and shrubs known to have been popular in the Roman period.

A fascinating exercise in recovery and preservation was initiated at about the same time as the excavations at Fishbourne, about 16 miles across the Sussex-Hampshire border near Portsmouth, and as a complex scientific project it

Although Chichester's importance increased after the removal of the bishopric from Selsey, its prominence as a regional centre lay in its position close to fertile country inland and to the penetrating inlets of the sea. Chichester's trade has been handled at least since Roman times by one or other of the small havens sheltering on these inlets – Itchenor, Birdham, Bosham and Dell Quay – formerly important shipbuilding or trading centres whose maritime activities today centre on yachts and yacht racing, their ancient waterfronts coloured with *Fireballs, Flying Dutchmen* and *505s*. Despite their popularity these sleepy anchorages retain an untouched quality – perhaps because they are visited by

will take years of painstaking work before it is complete. No museum can be built on this site, as at Fishbourne, for the find was Henry VIII's long-lost carrack the *Mary Rose*, and her resting place of more than 400 years had been soft mud six fathoms deep. The ship had lain on her side in a position unaltered, it is thought, since she heeled over without warning, with all her gun ports open, and sank on a stifling July day on her way to an engagement with the French Admiral d'Annebault's invading fleet. Entombed were the ship's captain, Roger Grenville, the vice-admiral Sir George Carew, the crew of about 500 freebooters, their personal possessions and all the paraphernalia of a Tudor fighting ship. The *Mary Rose* is particularly interesting for scholars because she was among the first of England's purpose-built fighting ships, specially created by Henry for his innovatory warfleet whose ships relied solely on gun battle and could keep a safe distance from their combatants. Until then, merchant ships were equipped with raised platforms – 'castles' – at strategic points where passengers and goods could be stowed, but which could be adapted for hand-to-hand fighting by soldiers as and when required. The full story of Henry's formidable fleet, and of the futuristic technology employed in 1982 to bring the hull unharmed to the surface and thereafter to preserve it, is now told in an exhibition mounted in Southsea Castle, which Henry had strengthened as part of his coastal defence system. It was from here that the King witnessed the demise of his favourite ship which he had named after his sister and which Sir Edward Howard had described as 'the flower I trow of all ships that ever sailed'.

It was Henry VIII who made Portsmouth the seat of England's naval power by creating the first permanent naval base here, and it was Lord Nelson who brought the town lasting glory by embarking for the fateful battle of Trafalgar in his flagship HMS *Victory*, which today is Portsmouth's most popular monument. The Admiral's last steps in England, pressed on all sides by tearful crowds, can be traced through some of the few thoroughfares in old Portsmouth that survived the 1940s air raids – a tangle of cobbled streets behind the waterfront where the eminent engineer Thomas Telford was born in 1757, and where further north Dickens' birthplace in Old Commercial Road can be visited as a museum. The Old Dockyard around the Main Gate and the ancient Hard has many eighteenth- and nineteenth-century buildings still in use, and they make an appropriate setting for Nelson's handsome ship which lies in dry dock, where visitors can see mementoes of Trafalgar, including the battle charts and the great man's cabin preserved in its original state. Nelson's departure from Portsmouth and its consequences may be thought the culmination of the town's greatest years as a naval base, although a considerable number of fortifications from all ages surround and reinforce the natural defences of its land-locked harbour. Palmerston, in the 1850s, built a line of impressive structures along the downs behind the town and even offshore, the furthest out being No Man's Land Fort. At the harbour entrance stands the medieval Round Tower, while a little to the south Henry V's Square Tower, built in the same period as Portsmouth's – and England's – first-ever dry dock, marks the first serious moves to base a navy here. After Henry's reign his navy was allowed to run down, and was the subject of a bitter lament, *The Libel of English Policy*, written by the Archbishop of Chichester, Adam de Moleyns, a minister of the crown: 'Where be our shippes, where be our swords become?' His end, ironically, was to be murdered in Portsmouth by discontented seamen. Even after Henry VIII had fortified Portsmouth and created his naval dockyards here, Leland commented in his *Itinerary*, 'The town is bare and little occupied in tyme of peace'. But from Tudor times the dockyards flourished, and today's harbour makes an invigorating scene of wharves, cranes, warships, freighters and pleasure yachts that can be sailed to the quiet, northerly reaches of Portsmouth Harbour where Portchester Castle stands with its twelfth-century church almost surrounded by water. The castle shows its powerful Roman wall and a formidable keep added by Henry II. Traces of a fourteenth-century tower remain, and of a palace built by Richard II and improved by Henry VIII; all this montage based on what is thought to have been *Portus Adurni*, one of the best-preserved of the Forts of the Saxon Shore.

The Romans had a fort, *Clausentium*, sited a few miles north-west on the river Itchen near Southampton. King Canute was offered the English crown (and also is said to have confronted the waves) here and a great castle was built soon after the Norman conquest, but it was the Middle Ages that saw Southampton's great days as a focus of trade and shipping, the south

Ancient walls of a vanished city: Southampton's Holy Rood Church, rebuilt in 1320, survived the widespread destruction of the city in the Second World War.

45

coast's premier medieval sea port. Large carracks from Genoa, and Venetian-owned 'Flanders Galleys', three-masted, with lateen rig and 180 oarsmen, nosed up Southampton Water toward the port, which is situated at a point where the estuaries of the rivers Test and Itchen meet. Silks, spices, wine and dyes were transported inland on the waters of the Itchen to Winchester and thence to London while wool, and later cloth, arrived at Southampton from the rich hinterland to make the return journey. The New Forest then clothed the shores of Southampton Water with oak, and medieval Southampton's shipyards were busy turning out merchantmen, or fitting them for battle. King John, Edward III and Henry V all amassed considerable war fleets here to sail from Southampton and Portsmouth against the French. Henry's fleet which in 1415 put out for Agincourt was, in terms of its unusual size and power, a forerunner of Henry VIII's navy – and both sovereigns had a *penchant* for massive ships that were prestigious rather than practical. The Tudor king's first *King Harry* was virtually unsailable and Henry V's then-unprecedented 1400-ton *Grace Dieu* proved too heavy to be sea-

worthy and was grounded in the mud off Bursledon, on the Hamble river, where her oaken timbers were visible until well into the present century.

From the middle of the nineteenth century when Southampton began to extend her docks to accommodate the world's growing steamships, the port again achieved the prominence of its medieval days – this time as a passenger link between London (by the newly-opened railway) and Mediterranean, Oriental and Atlantic routes:

weekly from Southampton great steamers white and gold
Go rolling down to Rio, roll down, roll down to Rio,
And I'd like to roll to Rio, some day before I'm old.

Within one century, Southampton was handling the world's most prestigious ocean

Southampton's formidable medieval walls surround a largely modern but historic city, England's premier port of the Middle Ages.

liners, and today combines rôles as home port for the *QE 2*, among others, and as a leading cargo and container port with modern docks built on reclaimed land which can accommodate container ships in excess of 300,000 tons. The dry docks where the Mulberry harbours of the Normandy landings were constructed now form a supply base for oil and gas exploration rigs in the Channel and South Western approaches. Few remnants of Southampton's hustling, warring, vigorous medieval life survived the 1940s raids, although a number of merchants' houses still stand in Porter's Lane, French Street and Simnel Street; the Wool House in Bugle Street holds the Maritime Museum, and the beginning of the Tudor period is marked by the fine Tudor House, built early in the sixteenth century. Substantial sections of the original city walls remain with immense gateways and towers, notably God's House Tower of the early fifteenth century and the Bargate, which dates from the twelfth century. Like a castle or cathedral the Bargate has been added to over varying periods so that it incorporates many towers and extensions, one of which is the Guildhall, strengthened and converted for use as a museum in the 1970s. An interesting twentieth-century exhibit is the D-Day embroidery, which traces Southampton's history through the Second World War when so much of Southampton's ancient centre was lost. In the post-war city there are many memorials, in particular of voyages that have been made from here – perhaps most stirring the Mayflower Memorial, and most tragic the plaque commemorating the departure of the *Titanic* in 1912 on her maiden voyage for New York. The Mayflower Park and the Royal Pier are vantage points for viewing Channel shipping where the steel giants of the twentieth century make their way along Southampton Water in the wake of skin-coated coracles, Flanders Galleys, luxury liners and sea-going craft from all the centuries between.

Other reminders of our maritime heritage are to be found on the waterside fringes of the New Forest around Southampton in tiny ports like Bucklers Hard on the Beaulieu River where some of the great merchant ships, the East Indiamen, were built – as they were at Itchenor on Chichester Harbour, and Bursledon on the Hamble. Huge oaken timbers were stacked to weather on the grass between Bucklers Hard's two sloping rows of cottages, and later the ships were launched from the same slipways as the *Illustrious*, the *Brilliant*, the *Agamemnon* – the 'wooden walls of Old England' and towed down-river for fitting out and final launching. In its heyday, this tiny village employed 4000 men. At the head of this lovely estuary is Beaulieu itself, still beautiful with its gabled waterside houses and Cistercian abbey ruin showing work from the thirteenth century onwards, and Lord Montagu's National Motor Museum in the grounds of Palace House, once the abbey's great gatehouse.

The westward coast along the Solent from Southampton Water to Lymington, pierced by the Beaulieu River, is lonely and beautiful, although dominated by the Fawley oil refinery whose flares light up the sky at night for miles around. Inland are the mysteries of the New Forest, stretches of desolate tawny heath, small woodland towns, forest ponies, deer. On the waters of the Solent are bright sails of yachts; liners, tankers, and the Lymington ferry which plies between Lymington and Yarmouth on the Isle of Wight – or lesser ferries making for Henry VIII's redoubtable Hurst Castle, marooned on a spit of shingle thrusting a mile and a half into the Channel. Lymington itself is the most lovely of the New Forest towns, an ancient salt-making place, its High Street rising between Georgian shopfronts to a grey church with tower and cupola, and cobbled Quay Hill tilting steeply down to the waterside. A weekend market contributes to the vitality of the town, and the Royal Lymington Yacht Club adds an exclusive touch. There are important boatyards with their own marinas, enclosed in massive pontoons moored along mudflats south of the town; mostly they produce pleasure and racing yachts, some of them world-class racers. The mudflats, despite the industry and activity, seem wild and untouched; ponies run untended here, and local people come to collect winkles. In early times these were the salterns, and they give a sense of continuity, perhaps because they are the working part of a town which supplied more fighting ships than Portsmouth in the Hundred Years' War. Lymington's boatyards also produce commercial vessels – pilot boats, dories, trawlers. These small boats and their Masters still form the backbone of the British fishing industry, despite competition from deep-sea trawlers and the economic pressures of today's industry. All along this coast, their craftsmanship, and the shipwrights', prolong a tradition of skill and stoicism that reaches beyond Roman or Celtic ages, into the forgotten recesses of time.

Overleaf Bucklers Hard on the Beaulieu river. This single-terrace Georgian village saw the construction of many great warships with their hearts – or hulls – of oak; among them, Lord Nelson's flagship *Agammemnon*.

4 Coast of Carved Stone

The natural harbour at Christchurch, Dorset. The town, which was mentioned in Domesday, grew at the head of the harbour where the rivers Avon and Stour converge.

The Dorset coastline is dramatic and strange, lonely, phenomenal. Home of the Purbeck Marblers and Hardy's 'Portland Slingers', stone hewers whose craft brought dark 'marble' pillars to our churches and creamy slabs of stone to build our cathedrals, its beauty spots are busy in the summer, but they are not built-up or close to holiday villages and seaside suburbs. Dorset holds the mystery of the Chesil bank and the Burning Cliff; the scenic marvels of scooped-out coves and of sculpted rocks in limestone or chalk; and one of the world's largest natural harbours, Poole. But since administrative changes in 1974 the eastward coastline has enclosed Mudeford, Christchurch and Bournemouth, with their evergreen suburbs, and

the sandy chines of Bournemouth Bay. This added coastline belongs to Hampshire in spirit, especially the quiet oyster- and winkle-dredging Mudeford, and Christchurch with its hump-backed bridge, tranquil river banks and boats. The Norman priory church dominates this old town more in presence than by visual means since its monastic bulk, shrouded in trees, is obscured by the winding street. Beyond are the remains of a Norman castle, and the waters of the lagoon-like harbour which are entered by the gentle rivers Avon and Stour. The seaward edge is shaped by the dog-leg promontory Hengistbury Head, mined for its ironstone in the Iron Ages, and with evidence of this ancient culture remaining in the form of round houses and a defensive double dyke that effectively cut Hengistbury off from land-based raids. From the headland can be seen Christchurch Bay's shallow cliffs of heath and pine spreading east toward Hurst Castle, and Bournemouth Bay curving to the distant built-up shoreline around Poole and the white cliffs of Purbeck. Facing Hengistbury

across the water are the Isle of Wight's glinting Needles, remnants of the far-off Purbeck Hills.

The Hampshire–Dorset border formerly fell between Bournemouth and Poole Harbour, the flooded river basin of the Frome. This 100 miles of ragged shoreline is clasped in the arms of Haven Point reaching north from Purbeck, and a spit of land called Sandbanks stretching south-westward from Bournemouth Bay to within 300 yards of the opposite shore. Further along north-west of Sandbanks, the port of Poole occupies its own natural harbour, busy with dockyards and boatbuilding and with marinas for holiday yachts. Poole is a town with a flamboyant history of piracy and smuggling. The ancient centre – Market Street, Church Street, and some parts of High Street – is preserved amid a confusion of arterial roads and apartment blocks, and is now known as the Old Town. On the busy quay the fine nineteenth-century Custom House and Harbour Office of 1727, and old pubs and wharves, remind us of what used to be. Poole has always flourished as a working town, and at the

Brownsea Island at the mouth of Poole Harbour is a peaceful retreat with woodland, a castle and pleasant shores for holidaymakers. Part of the island holds a nature reserve administered by the National Trust.

Leisure and industry around Sandbanks, Poole Harbour. Britain's largest natural harbour is rich in wildlife, provides sandy beaches and marinas and continues its tradition as a busy trading centre for small ships.

end of the last century, when the Newfoundland fishing trade had finally failed, the town began to export clay from alluvial deposits around the harbour, and built its own successful pottery business which is popular with today's visitors. For visitors who come in small dinghies those extensive harbour shores must be fascinating to explore, particularly on the lonely Purbeck fringe where numerous waterfowl nest among islets and inlets silted with mud and Spartina grass. Purbeck marble and clay used to be off-loaded from here until the jetties were deserted by the waters, and in turn deserted by their owners. Just inside the 300-yard harbour entrance lies the National Trust's Brownsea Island, a square mile of heath and woodland where the red squirrel survives, and where the ruins of one of Henry VIII's castles guards the harbour approach. Brownsea's former owners have put the island to various and eccentric uses, but it is also gratefully remembered as the site of Lord Baden-Powell's first scout camp. Situated just inside the narrow mouth of the harbour, the island does nothing to ease the life of yachtsmen trying to avoid the sandbanks and other irritations. For Hilaire

Belloc in his *Voyage of the Nona* the entrance was 'a trap, baited and set'; and he wondered how the ancients managed without the brightly-lit buoys and other aids of the present age.

The Romans knew the area, for a slab of Purbeck marble carved in dedication to Minerva and Neptune was dug up early in the seventeenth century, and can be seen set into a wall of Poole's colonnaded Council House. The Saxons certainly used Poole Harbour, although they would find it altered today. The sleepy town of Wareham, situated a mile or so along the River Frome, once stood at the westward extent of the tidal basin which formed the river valley in earlier times, and it was the harbour's main port until the Middle Ages. Today, Wareham's peaceful skyline makes a pleasant entry into the Purbeck peninsula for those travelling along the A351 from Poole; it is a predominantly Georgian town whose pre-conquest church is the oldest in Dorset, and whose quiet streets and riverside walks belie its turbulent beginnings as a Saxon stronghold on shores that were under constant threat from Scandinavian marauders. It was from Wareham that the enemy entered Exeter overland – and, it

is thought, it was on these shores that King Alfred built England's first-recorded navy – his fleet of 'swifter, steadier' ships.

The main road, bisecting the squarish Purbeck peninsula, heads for Corfe Castle which occupies a gap in the narrow Purbeck range that arcs from the east to the south coast. The sudden view of this dark ruin on its height, flanked by the shoulders of the Purbeck Hills, gives an idea of the site's strategic importance to the Saxon kings who fortified the hill on which the Norman structure stands. It is an awesome ruin, with a history of foul deeds, brooding over a green pastoral countryside. Its end came in the Civil War when it was besieged, and fell to the Roundheads after a protracted and valiant resistance by the widow of Sir John Bankes. Much of the Purbeck stone that formed its fabric went into the houses of Corfe village, which look across at the stark remains from their own small hill. In medieval times there was a marble-carving industry here, evident in the stonework shown in some of the old houses, and this feeling of domestic stability makes contrast with the haunted atmosphere of the castle. Even its site is

touched with tragedy, for it was built near the Saxon hunting lodge where Edward the Martyr was stabbed in the back on orders of his stepmother who wanted the crown for Ethelred the Unready, her son:

> No worse deed for the English was ever done
>   Than this was,
> Since first they came to the land of Britain...

Swanage, quarrying town turned pleasure resort, also features in the *Anglo-Saxon Chronicle*: '...and the pirate host sailed west about, and they were caught in a great storm at sea, and there off Swanage one hundred and twenty ships were lost'. This misfortune, and a victorious sea-battle under King Alfred that preceded it, are commemorated on the seafront by a tall column erected in 1863 by John Mowlem of the local stone contracting firm, Mowlem & Burt. Sydney Heath, writing about the Dorset coast in 1910, comments, 'the obelisk is surmounted by three "cannon-balls", the introduction of which to commemorate a battle fought in the ninth century is surely carrying artistic licence a little too far'. Sheltered in the wide curve of Swanage Bay, on a coast of white cliffs and

On the Purbeck peninsula the shady village of Studland with its Norman church nestles behind low cliffs and sandy beaches while the old town of Swanage offers the more robust pleasures of the seaside resort.

Held in the limestone arms of the Purbeck and Portland series, Lulworth Cove is famed as a beauty spot and geologists' paradise; formerly it was the haunt of pirates and smugglers.

glorious golden sands, this predominantly Victorian resort was liberally embellished through the efforts of Mowlem & Burt, presumably to bring it into line with sophisticated places like Bournemouth. Charles Harper, also writing in the early 1900s, devoted a chapter to the 'Oddities of Swanage': the Gothic clock tower (lacking its clock) brought from London Bridge to Swanage Pier; a flying-fish weather vane surmounting the archaic tower of Burt's Purbeck House, massive Gothic, which stands opposite the Town Hall; the Wren facade of the Town Hall, taken brick by brick from the Mercers' Hall in Cheapside. Far removed from Saxon sea battles and from the refined sophistications of Bournemouth, Swanage makes a comfortable base from which to discover the extraordinary beauties of the Dorset cliffs.

The main road ends at, or starts with, Swanage – but another route starts nearby, and that is the South-West Peninsula Coast Path which runs for 500 miles between Haven Point, where the Poole ferries arrive, to Minehead in Somerset. The Haven Point end of the path makes a fine introduction to any ramble, whether it be the ten miles or so to Swanage, or the full 500 miles to Somerset. The dunes and heaths of the Studland peninsula drop away as the path climbs the 390-foot chalk outcrop of Ballard Down to offer views stretching across the sea as far as the Solent and the Isle of Wight on clear days, and southward past beautiful Swanage Bay to Durlston Head. The Old Harry Rocks isolated at the foot of the cliff are the weird, white legacy of the drowned and eroded hills that once extended to the Isle of Wight. Behind the coastal panorama the downs roll away across the Purbeck Hills that emerge at Worbarrow Bay along Purbeck's southern coast. It is the Jurassic limestone deposits laid down in the wedge of land between the arc of these hills and the coast that are quarried for building stone. In the Vale of Purbeck, under the shelter of the

400 feet above the sea, stands a strong, square Norman chapel with a single central pillar supporting the vaulted ceiling and a slit window cut into the massive thickness of the eastern wall. Just inland are the quarryman's villages, and fields edged with drystone walls. Nearest to St Aldhelm's is Worth Matravers, built in the shelter of a hill, with a fine Norman church standing on Saxon foundations. Here existed a society which allowed stoneworking skills to be passed only from father to son, and work allotted only to those who, after a seven-year apprenticeship, became Fellows of the Ancient Order of Purbeck Marblers & Stonecutters. Although this regulation has been obsolete for more than a century, stoneworkers can still apply to join the order.

Walkers from either direction, crossing St Aldhelm's Head, look back at a long sweep of dramatic cliffs and forward to a fresh view that is equally fine. Following westward, the limestone cliffs carved by man are superseded by an alternating sequence of clays and limestone and chalk, scoured away by the action of rain, wind and waves. First come Chapman's Pool, a bay scooped from cliffs of crumbly black Kimmeridge clay, and then a chaotic stretch, the Kimmeridge Ledges, alternating horizontal strata of soft eroded clay and hard limestone, where the rocks lie in a tumbled mass along the strand. This, too, is a working coast, and at sheltered Kimmeridge Bay British Petroleum's small oil wells are the modern equivalents of former attempts, some bizarre, to exploit the fuel content of 'Kimmeridge Coal'. Iron Age people made armlets of the shaly clay, and the discarded centres left mysterious discs which have only recently been explained. Over the next six miles the coast may be followed only for 48 weeks in the year, because it is used as an Army shooting range. Here is an introduction to some of Dorset's most impressive coastal scenery, beginning at the towering limestone mass of Gad's Cliff and continuing into the curve of eroded coastline where the waves have worn into the limestone cliff to reveal, at Worbarrow Bay and Mupe Bay, a shallow crescent of clay, then chalk, then clay and limestone. Further westward, the limestone is breached to make Lulworth Cove.

This was formed in the same way as the curve at Worbarrow and Mupe Bays, but the gap in the limestone is very narrow and the waves have scooped out a small rounded cove beyond. The colours of the sailing boats and the animation of the holiday crowds may seem at odds with the

hills, lies the upper stratum of the Purbeck series which yields the dark, grey-green 'marble' so popular in the thirteenth-century churches of England – laid down in primaeval lakes principally from the shells of freshwater snails. From Durlston Head to St Aldhelm's Head along the first south-westward stretch of the Purbeck coast, at Tilly Whim caves, along Dancing Ledge, at Seacombe and Winspit, one can see the pillared caverns or the ledges that have been cut into the lower cliff face to win the creamy Purbeck-Portland freestone of the lower stratum. Durlston Head is decked out with more 'oddities' from the Mowlem & Burt collection, notably a vast stone globe of the world, and various stone texts and scripts, to remind us of where some of the profit went from the exertions of the stone workers who carved these Dorset cliffs. On the eastern flank of St Aldhelm's Head one can see the work of earlier people in the Celtic field system still visible under the turf and here, almost

lyrical beauties of turf-topped, white cliffs, white pebbles, and blue-green of water encircled by stone. But Lulworth, always a sheltered haven for fishing boats, was once the haunt of pirates and smugglers – and has had an eventful past. Just to the east, back within Army territory at the base of Bindon Hill, a fragment of a fossilised forest is visible above the high tide mark. Across the rearing westward headland is the contorted cliff formation of Stair Hole, showing the scooping action of the waves on a miniature scale while graphically illustrating the folding and tipping of the land which occurred during the protracted earth movements that uplifted the Alps. It is as exciting visually as geologically, particularly when angry waves surge back and forth, spray is thrown up, and winds howl. The whole cliff sequence westward is one of wild grandeur culminating in another geological and scenic marvel, Durdle Door, a jagged white limestone arch projecting into the sea from high chalk cliffs backed by the Chaldon Downs. From here the chalk or limestone cliffs range tall until White Nothe, 500 feet of chalk, marks the change to

older rocks. Ringstead Bay, sheltered by White Nothe's eastward bulk, is carved from dark Kimmeridge clays. On the Holworth cliffs here a slow-moving landslip of the 1820s was said to have removed intact a cottage complete with garden 200 feet down the cliff, over a period of three years. A further phenomenon took the form of a sulphurous burning of the cliff top, which was thought to have been the result of spontaneous combustion of the bituminous shale, and caused consternation and excitement for a number of years. From White Nothe, where the whole of the coast from St Aldhelm's Head to Portland Bill and beyond spreads below, the cliffs subside past Osmington Mills and into the curve of Weymouth Bay.

The Isle of Portland consists of limestone in its upper layer and this is rugged and craggy, but the surface has been eroded by men rather than by waves. Like the Isle of Purbeck, Portland is famous for its building stone; like Purbeck it is not an isle, but its people traditionally have thought of themselves as a race apart, and once conformed to strict conventions that kept them so. Unlike Purbeck, Portland is tiny – an uptilted wedge of land that is linked to the 'adjacent island of Great Britain' by a thin strip carrying the main road from Weymouth, and by the long, lonely storm beach, the Chesil bank, for eight miles separated from the land by two narrow lagoons, East and West Fleet. Since the mid-nineteenth century, Hardy's 'Gibraltar of Wessex' has been occupied by the Navy and by a prison which was established to provide a workforce for building the vast naval base on Portland's north-east flank at a time when the French were building Cherbourg out of similar mistrust. The harbour took six million tons of the stone that built Inigo Jones' Banqueting House in Whitehall, and Wren's St Paul's Cathedral, and with which Portland's white villages and towns glare on hot days amid a treeless landscape of boulders and patchy heath. Castletown, steeply built on Portland's northern edge, combines the sobriety of an industrial settlement with the dazzle of a Mediterranean hill-town as the land rises a dramatic 496 feet from harbour and road before declining over the next four-and-a half miles to its tip, the Bill of Portland. One of Henry VIII's castles high over the harbour stares across Weymouth Bay while to the north-west lies the ever-receding strip of Chesil Beach, caught between the blue of the sea and the East and West Fleets gleaming in the green of the land.

Chesil Beach is not so much spectacular or odd as a phenomenon that has yet to be explained. It comprises an 18-mile bank of pebbles neatly graded in colour and circumference from yellow-brown pea-size near Bridport to greyish, fist-size at Portland, where the shingle (called by the Saxons *cisel*) reaches a height of 45 feet. 'Steepstone Bank' has been built by the sea on a bed of Kimmeridge clay with pebbles that come from as far west as Cornwall. Fishermen and, in former days, smugglers, have claimed to recognise their location in the dark according to the size of the pebbles and their sound in the surf. The surf can be treacherous, for the coastline here takes the full force of south-westerly gales, and has claimed many ships and lives, earning the grim title 'Deadman's Bay'. The beach, uncomfortable and dangerous, is empty apart from fishing boats. Below the village of Abbotsbury, where the brackish waters of West Fleet end, Chesil becomes part of the foreshore, and clumps of pine darken the skyline of hills that rise from tamarisk-fringed shingle, narrow pastures, and stone farm buildings. Examples of Saxon strip-farming are visible near St Catherine's Chapel, which stands on a windswept mound between Abbotsbury village and its swannery on the shores of the West Fleet.

Created by the village's now-vanished monastery, the swannery has varieties of geese and ducks as well as over 500 swans. An old rhyme gives a recipe that may or may not have been used by the monks of Abbotsbury:

To a gravy of beef, good and strong, I opine,
You'll be right if you add half a pint of port wine;
Pour this through the swan – yes, quite through the
    belly,
Then serve the whole up with some hot currant jelly.

Different lines were murmured by Abbotsbury maidens under the vaulted roof of St Catherine's Chapel:

A handsome one, St Catherine,
A rich one, St Catherine,
A nice one, St Catherine,
But one of some sort, if you please,
And soon, St Catherine.

Like St Aldhelm's Chapel St Catherine's is beautiful in its simplicity and massively buttressed, although it is larger and more elaborate. It dates from the fifteenth century, and was built as a seamen's chapel; perhaps the seamen provided answers to the maidens' prayers. The village of thatched and slated-roofed cottages stands a little to the north, and the pulpit in the parish church still carries the scars of the Civil War when in 1644 Royalist forces were attacked by Parliamentarians under Sir Anthony Ashley Cooper who later reported, 'We...sent them a summons by a trumpeter, to which they returned a slighting answer and hung out their bloody flag. Immediately we drew out a party of musketeers, with which Major Bainton in person stormed the church....This, after a hot bickering, we carried....' The reed-thatched tithe barn of the Benedictine Abbey which was founded around 1026 survives to the south; westward near the sea are sub-tropical gardens, and to the north-west stands an Iron Age fort. From here the road toward Burton Bradstock and Bridport bounces over unfolding vistas of serried hills, the rolling contours of the ridge following high above, the long sea-girt stretch of Chesil far below. At any time of the day or the year this makes one of the loveliest drives in England. Distant are the last of Dorset's colourful cliffs – Golden Cap rising west of Chideock, Black Ven to the west of Charmouth – and the Devon coast beyond.

5 Former Glories

The rugged landscapes of Purbeck and Portland produced closed societies whose skills live on in the soaring towers and pillars of England's cathedrals. Devon's deep estuaries and vivid cliffs, clothed in fields and woods, nurtured seafarers who crossed the ocean for cod – and for ivory, pepper, and gold. Early in the sixteenth century, William Hawkins of Plymouth had sailed to the Ivory Coast and to Brazil, where the Portuguese traded but no English ship had ever been. Throughout the latter half of the century, Dartmouth and Plymouth were leading ports in the Newfoundland cod trade, sending fleets across the Atlantic to spend the summers harvesting the rich waters there. This arduous and profitable industry grew up at a time when the west-countrymen John Hawkins, Drake, Raleigh and others were upholding the Protestant cause, and championing Queen and country in the quarrel with Catholic Spain. Great personal fortunes could be made by carrying on an informal war by privateering – a Channel tradition of legalised piracy that had stood the test of time since the days of the great Cinque Ports. The Plymouth-based ships were often commissioned by the Huguenots or by the Orange republic, if not by the Queen. The adventurers rode rough-shod over the waves of the Spanish Main, and brought home in their frail ships treasure almost beyond price. Raleigh founded the colony of Virginia, Drake 'singed the King of Spain's beard' at Cadiz, Hawkins fitted out England's fleet of small ships in readiness for the Armada when it came: these famous sea rovers and their ships gilded the history of England with their deeds – bloodstained but none the less celebrated – and with their names.

Other deeds were performed by forgotten heroes all along the coast, as they are today. The selfless acts of courage performed by lifeboat crews, and the individual bravery of villagers in assisting victims of wrecks, were less celebrated but no less noteworthy – even if there was also gain involved for the villagers from salving lost cargoes. As for the smugglers – every seaside village must have had its Hawkins, Drake or Raleigh in the seventeenth and eighteenth centuries. Even though the illustrious names carried out their deeds under contract, while the 'Gentlemen' were outside the law, the work of bringing home the brandy, tobacco or fine silks involved the same skills of seamanship, the same bravado and the same brutal treatment of those who stood in the adventurers' way. Travelling westward along the Devon coast, one imagines this vigorous lifestyle set against the arresting beauties of sea, cliff and combe. Between the estuaries of the rivers Axe and Exe, the sudden change from white cliffs to red can be seen on either side from Beer Head, over 400 feet above the sea. Below are smugglers' caves – and a local man of the nineteenth century, Jack Rattenbury, is remembered in Devon for the book he wrote about his exploits when he was no longer fit enough to profit by them. Nearby is a well-known beauty spot, the fishing village of Beer, once known for lace making as well as for smuggling. Beer's craftswomen supplied the lace for Queen Victoria's wedding dress – but it is the smugglers who are remembered. Further along this part of the coast between Sidmouth and Budleigh Salterton is another beauty spot, Ladram Bay, encircled by red cliffs and with craggy rocks jutting out of the sea. The modest resort of Budleigh Salterton, genteel and verdant, was the setting for John Millais' romantic painting *The Boyhood of Raleigh*, and it was just a mile or so inland at Hayes Barton Farm, surrounded by

Devon fields and lanes, that Raleigh was born. Across the western headland the coast turns and the broad estuary of the river Exe, with Exmouth on its eastern bank, leads inland to Devon's capital, Exeter, with its outport of Roman times, Topsham, situated four miles downstream. This quiet riverside town once rivalled Dartmouth in the number of ships it sent to Newfoundland, and later launched East Indiamen from its boatyards. Now it dozes on the river bank with its forgotten dockyards, its eighteenth-century Dutch cloth merchants' houses along the Strand, and some good pubs – part of Exeter, yet still unspoiled.

Brixham too is unspoiled, its houses steeply crowded on the harbourside at the westward edge of Torbay, still thriving as a fishing town. For the nineteenth-century historian Lord Macaulay, describing William of Orange's arrival there, Brixham was the 'wealthiest seat of our fishing trade', and much changed since the Protestant king landed in 1688: 'Where we now see a port crowded with shipping, and a marketplace swarming with buyers and sellers, the waves then broke on a desolate beach'. The magnificent fleet of trawlers that operated in Lord Macaulay's time has gone, but the fishing boats still crowd the harbour, the fish market for traders makes an energetic scene, and for holidaymakers an aquarium stands opposite while Brixham's floodlit caverns, discovered a year after Macaulay's death in 1859, rival those of Torquay.

Dartmouth's age of prosperity is reflected in the seventeenth-century buildings which survive in the older corners of the town, notably the arcaded Buttermarket, which is perhaps the finest example – the granite pillars giving an undeniably west-country touch. There are good period buildings in Bayard's Cove, where there is a remnant of a Henry VIII castle, and in Anzac and Higher Street, both near St Saviour's Church. Here can be seen the heraldic shields of the town's merchant adventurers preserved among the church's wealth of furnishings from the fourteenth to the seventeenth centuries. Particularly rich is the carving of the sixteenth-century stone pulpit – vivid in its painting and gilding – or the ironwork of the south door, full of vitality, whose date of 1631 appears in the design, although its rampant beasts are thought to be older. In the chancel is a brass grouping of John Hawley and his two wives. Seven times mayor, this fourteenth-century town worthy is sometimes suggested as the model for the Shipman in Chaucer's *Canterbury Tales*:

A Shipman was ther woning fer by weste
For aught I woot he was of Dertemouthe.

Hawley's large fleet of merchantmen inspired a local rhyme:

Blowe the wynd high, blowe the wynd low,
It bloweth goode to Hawley's hoe.

Dartmouth was one of England's leading ports in medieval times, trading in wool, cloth and wine. Pilgrims arrived from Europe to visit Becket's shrine, and set off for the shrine of St James of Compostela in Spain. The fleets sailing to the second and third Crusades in the twelfth century assembled here from both sides of the Channel, and in 1346 the town sent 31 ships to the siege of Calais. A castle was built at the mouth of the river, and one at Kingswear on the other side, late in the fifteenth century, and a chain could be stretched between to prevent entry. In 1592 Raleigh's carrack *Madre de Dios* came in, loaded with perfumes, pepper and precious stones, and Raleigh had to be released from the Tower to salve what he might for himself and the Queen before the crew took what they could, and melted into the countryside. Dartmouth's vitality

Brooding over its village from an adjacent hill, the ruin of Corfe Castle makes a dramatic silhouette across the rich pastoral countryside around the Purbeck Hills.

as a seaport did not subside until the final days of the Newfoundland cod trade, and late in the nineteenth century it was decided to base the Royal Naval College here. In 1905 a grand spread of college buildings took shape on a hillside dominating the town. A travel writer of the time commented, 'it is designed in the Paltry Picturesque Eclectic Renaissance or Doll's House, style with ornamental fripperies and fandangalums galore', but then continued in more encouraging tones, 'the long range of buildings, backed by dark trees, sets just that crown and finish upon Dartmouth which suffices to raise the scenic character of the place from beauty to nobility'. Dartmouth standing on its estuary could certainly have no lovelier setting than this winding water renowned for its beauty, scattered with sailing boats, penetrating the woods and fields in the calm of rural Devon. Her face is her fortune these days, but although like other south coast seaports she is a holiday place as well as a working town, there is much to remind us of the adventurous, golden, cruel age when a voyage would as likely lose you life and limb as earn you fish, spice, silks or gold.

Plymouth is a substantial city enclosed on all sides by winding estuaries across which can be seen river banks of fields or woods. During the Elizabethan period it was one of England's four most important towns, and it became the base of the English Navy, largely through the adventuring of local families or individuals. The eastern flank occupies the banks of the Cattewater, an estuary that enters Plymouth Sound from the north east, and the western edge borders the Hamoaze – a continuation of the Tamar estuary that reaches further inland. The southern shore of historic Plymouth looks out on the Sound, a broad mouth of water entering the Channel through Cawsand Bay and held between the west and east coasts of Devon and Cornwall. From Plymouth's naval dockyards at Devonport on the Hamoaze the Torpoint Ferry plies between the two counties, and further up the estuary the modern Tamar road bridge spans the divide alongside Brunel's magnificent rail bridge of 1859. This combination of power and grace opened new routes far into Cornwall and began the process of Anglicisation in the county where people will still assure you that Plymouth is the first and last

Old Plymouth: Sutton
Harbour, where
fishermen come to sell
their catch and where
visitors can savour the
atmosphere of ancient
days.

town on the Channel coast of England. In Drake's day, for many, Plymouth became one of the First towns of all England.

A flavour of former glories lingers in Plymouth's Barbican, part of Drake's city that survived the 1940s bombing raids. Old buildings edge Sutton Harbour where fishing boats and sailing yachts are moored, and the sounds and savours of a busy fish market permeate the waterside pubs, the boutiques and the narrow alleyways. In New Street one can visit a fine Elizabethan house, gabled and with oriel windows, restored early this century and furnished in period. In 1620, Island House, at the harbour end of the street, provided the last lodgings in England for some of the 102 emigrants who set sail in their elderly merchant ship the *Mayflower* to found the colony of New England from the point now called the Mayflower Steps. Later to become known as the

Pilgrim Fathers, the emigrants, who were fleeing religious persecution, are commemorated on a plaque outside Island House on which their names are listed – men, women and children. The *Mayflower's* sister ship *Speedwell*, which was in even worse repair and had been the cause of a series of false starts (the company had originally sailed from Southampton), had to be abandoned in Plymouth with her passengers and crew.

Plymouth's post-war commercial centre, rising from the ashes of the old, has some good modern buildings, although overall it shares the prosaic character of twentieth-century towns. There is an attractive and entertaining domed fruit and vegetable market at the western end, and some of the more interesting buildings include the Council House and the Law Courts, just south of the pedestrianised shopping centre. Near here are two remnants of the old city, a merchant's house of the mid-sixteenth century, a substantial building with a fine and elaborate twin-gabled façade, and Prysten House – a lodging place for Augustinian monks from Plympton Priory visiting St Andrew's Church – powerful and simple in contrast to the much-embellished merchant's house, and with a pretty courtyard. St Andrew's like the nearby Guildhall was well restored after the blitz, the original granite pillars bearing new arches, the floors laid with Delabole slate, and John Piper's windows vibrant at the east end of the church. This was one of the Plymouth churches whose congregations abandoned their worship one Sunday in 1573 to witness the return of Drake and his two small ships from the Isthmus of Panama bringing with him stories of amazing adventure and plunder worth £40,000. One of his first successful raids, it heralded the rise of Drake's career from independent privateer to 'General of her Majesty's Navy', who helped defeat the great Armada and thereby establish England's supremacy as a naval power. After his round-the-world voyage in the *Golden Hind* from 1577 to 1580, on his return at Deptford with his shipful of treasure, Drake was knighted; Plymouth made him its mayor. His figure, cast in bronze, today contemplates Drake's Island and Plymouth Sound from the sweeping, spacious sward of the windswept Hoe – his right hand resting lightly but proprietorially on the globe which he was the first captain to circumnavigate. Just behind his statue, in Hoe Park, one can still enjoy a game of bowls.

Plymouth's Victorian suburbs are built of granite and slate, and of the handsome, greyish-pink limestone that outcrops on Plymouth Hoe. This was the material used for Charles II's formidable Citadel, situated south of the Barbican and east of the Hoe, occupying the corner of land where Sutton Harbour opens into Plymouth Sound. In 1671, less than a century after England's defeat of the Armada, Charles II and his brother sailed from Dover in their pleasure yacht to see the new fortress, built to keep order in Protestant Plymouth with gun positions directed over the town as well as over the water. Less than 20 years later this precaution was rendered unnecessary when Dutch William deposed Charles's brother, James II. The law-abiding citizens of today can visit the aquarium that stands beside Charles's assertive fortress, and is also occupied by the laboratories of the Marine Biological Association. This is England's principal marine biological research centre, and has its own research vessels moored in the

civilian port of Millbay, just west of the Hoe. By the waterside, south of the Citadel, is the headquarters of the Royal Corinthian Yacht Club, and on West Hoe's Grand Parade is the club house of the Royal Western Yacht Club of England. This provides present-day drama by organising major international events from Plymouth like the Round-the-World, Transatlantic or Round-Britain races.

All of the great sailors of Elizabeth I's Plymouth were involved in the routing of the Spanish Armada in 1588. The fleet of fast, low-built, manoeuvrable ships was assembled in Plymouth by the Treasurer of the Queen's Navy John Hawkins; his elderly brother William, then Plymouth's mayor, supervised their scraping and tallowing. The Armada's eventual arrival off the Cornish coast was unexpected, but the English put out from Plymouth at sunset, and got to westward of the Spanish fleet. The light, summery, westerly wind blew both fleets up-Channel past the Sound, past the still-lonely, dark and rugged rocks from Plymouth to Bolt Head, past the Kingsbridge estuary, still lovely, winding and serene, with Salcombe embedded in cypresses and pines on the western bank; and in the wake of the combatants we retrace our steps along all of England's south coast, past Weymouth, where the coastal watchers saw action, as they did off the Isle of Wight; off the Owers Shoal, where the Armada narrowly escaped grounding, and across to Calais, where at midnight the English fireships went in. Here we retrace the steps of history also, for 23 miles across the water at Dover 1600 years earlier Caesar's men in their small ships saw 'the enemy posted on all the hills' – and almost 2000 years after that Dover became the centre of operations for another fleet of small ships, commandeered from every creek and haven of the Channel coast, which rescued 25,000 British soldiers and half as many French from the beaches of Dunkirk.

One year after the defeat of the Armada in 1588, the chronicler Richard Hakluyt could write at length on the widened horizons of Elizabeth's reign:

What English ship did heretofore ever anchor in the mighty river of Plate? Pass and repass the unpassable (in former opinion) strait of Magellan, range along the coast of Chili, Peru and all the backside of Nova Hispania, further than any Christian ever passed, traverse the mighty breadth of the South Sea, land upon the Luzones, in despite of the enemy, enter into alliance, amity and traffic with the Princes of Maluccas,

Plymouth Hoe. Sir Francis Drake's reputed bowling ground is marked by Smeaton's Tower, the original red-and-white striped Eddystone lighthouse. To the right is the Citadel built by Charles II.

and the isle of Java, double the famous Cape of Bona Speranza, arrive at the isle of St Helena, and last of all return home richly laden with the commodities of China, as the subjects of this now flourishing monarch have done?

In this century these strange places can be reached by plane, and are visited by ordinary men and women who have no notion of seamanship. Are they as strange to us today as the south coast of the twentieth century might seem to Hakluyt? He would see those of us who are not jet-hopping to the Canaries, or hitch-hiking to India, sun soaking in deckchairs at Eastbourne and listening to the brass under the brilliant blue curve of the bandstand; wind-surfing off Beachy Head, or being taken out from Swanage by fishermen in their plastic boats to a 'dive' on the charted wrecks, clad in wetsuit and fins, air bottles on our backs; or queuing up to drive into the mouth of the monster hovercraft before riding on a cloud of spray to the Isle of Wight, or France. To the first Elizabethans the south coast – shipping highway, fishing ground and pleasure park – would seem as strange, perhaps, as Hakluyt's Nova Hispania, or mighty Plate. To us, and our visitors, it must remain one of England's most varied, exciting and beautiful four hundred miles of coast.